Zaner-Bloser
Handwriting
With continuous-stroke alphabet

2M

Author

Clinton S. Hackney

Contributing Authors

Pamela J. Farris

Janice T. Jones

Linda Leonard Lamme

Zaner-Bloser, Inc.

P.O. Box 16764

Columbus, Ohio 43216-6764

Author

Clinton S. Hackney, Ed.D.

Contributing Authors

Pamela J. Farris, Ph.D.
Janice T. Jones, M.A.
Linda Leonard Lamme, Ph.D.

Reviewers

Judy L. Bausch, Columbus, Georgia

Cherlynn Bruce, Conroe, Texas

Karen H. Burke, Director of Curriculum and Instruction, Bar Mills, Maine

Anne Chamberlin, Lynchburg, Virginia

Carol J. Fuhler, Flagstaff, Arizona

Deborah D. Gallagher, Gainesville, Florida

Kathleen Harrington, Redford, Michigan

Rebecca James, East Greenbush, New York

Gerald R. Maeckelbergh, Principal, Blaine, Minnesota

Bessie B. Peabody, Principal, East St. Louis, Illinois

Marilyn S. Petruska, Coraopolis, Pennsylvania

Sharon Ralph, Nashville, Tennessee

Linda E. Ritchie, Birmingham, Alabama

Roberta Hogan Royer, North Canton, Ohio

Marion Redmond Starks, Baltimore, Maryland

Elizabeth J. Taglieri, Lake Zurich, Illinois

Claudia Williams, Lewisburg, West Virginia

Credits

Art: Lizi Boyd: 1, 6, 22–23, 28–29, 36–37, 54, 84–85, 99–100; Denise & Fernando: 3–4, 6, 20–21, 34–35, 68–69, 86–87, 100; Gloria Elliott: 5, 16, 42; Michael Grejniec: 4, 7, 11, 24–25, 30–31, 60–61, 76–77, 92–93, 101; Shari Halpern: 3, 6, 26–27, 32–33, 38–39, 44–45, 52, 72–73, 82, 96–97, 100; Daniel Moreton: 43, 53, 71, 81; Diane Paterson: 88–89; Andy San Diego: 3, 4, 6, 46–47, 56–57, 64–65, 80, 100; Troy Viss: 4–5, 7, 16, 42, 48–49, 58–59, 66–67, 74–75, 94–95, 101

Photos: John Lei/OPC: 8–9; Stephen Ogilvy:3–5, 10, 12–19, 23, 26–27, 32–33, 40–43, 45–47, 50, 52, 54–59, 62–63, 68–70, 74–78, 80–87, 90–91, 94–97, 99

Developed by Kirchoff/Wohlberg, Inc., in cooperation with Zaner-Bloser Publishers

Cover illustration by Lizi Boyd

ISBN 0-88085-946-6

01 02 DP 8 7

Copyright © 1999 Zaner-Bloser, Inc.

Zaner-Bloser, Inc., P.O. Box 16764, Columbus, Ohio 43216-6764, 1-800-421-3018

Printed in the United States of America

CONTENTS

Getting Started

Writing in Manuscript

Keys to Legibility

Follow the path. Write each letter you find.

What can the letters spell?
Write the word and read the message.

Let's _____.

In this book, you will find letters, words, and sentences to write. You will learn how to make your manuscript writing easy for you and for others to read.

5

I Can
I can write a story.
I can write a poem.
I can write at school,
And I can write at home.

I Can
I can write a story.
I can write a poem.
I can write at school,
And I can write at home.

I Can

I can write a story.

I can write a poem.

I can write at school,

And I can write at home.

I Can
I can write a story.
I can write a poem.
I can write at school,
And I can write at home.

I Can

I can write a story.
I can write a poem.
I can write at school,
And I can write at home.

Write the poem in your best handwriting.

Put a star next to your best line of writing.

7

Left-Handed Writers

If you write with your left hand...

Slant your paper. Pull your downstrokes toward your left elbow.

Hold your pencil with your first two fingers and thumb. Point the pencil toward your left elbow.

Sit up tall. Place both arms on the table. Keep your feet flat on the floor.

Right-Handed Writers

If you write with your right hand . . .

Keep your paper straight. Pull your downstrokes toward the middle of your body.

Hold your pencil with your first two fingers and thumb. Point the pencil toward your right shoulder.

Sit up tall. Place both arms on the table. Keep your feet flat on the floor.

Letters and Numerals

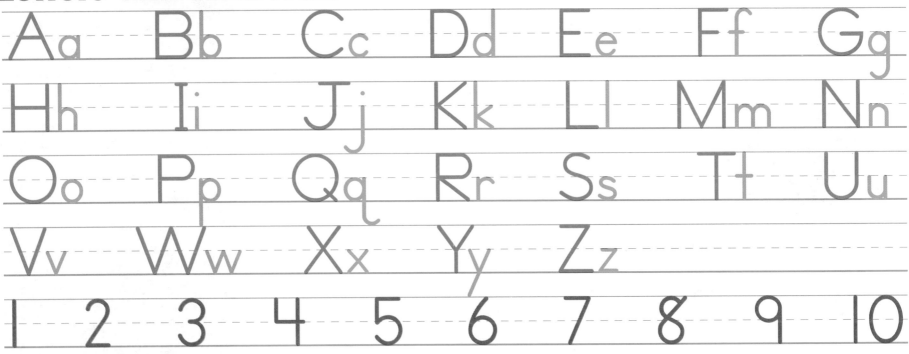

A a   B b   C c   D d   E e   F f   G g

H h   I i   J j   K k   L l   M m   N n

O o   P p   Q q   R r   S s   T t   U u

V v   W w   X x   Y y   Z z

1   2   3   4   5   6   7   8   9   10

Circle the letters you use to write your name.

Circle the numeral that tells your age.

Tall letters touch the headline.
All uppercase letters are tall.
Circle the tall letters.

b c d D v F h m

Short letters touch the midline.
Circle the short letters.

a c f i P n o

Some letters go below the baseline.
Circle the letters that go below the baseline.

g j G p q y x X

Write your name. Remember to begin with an uppercase letter.

Write the age you will be on your next birthday.

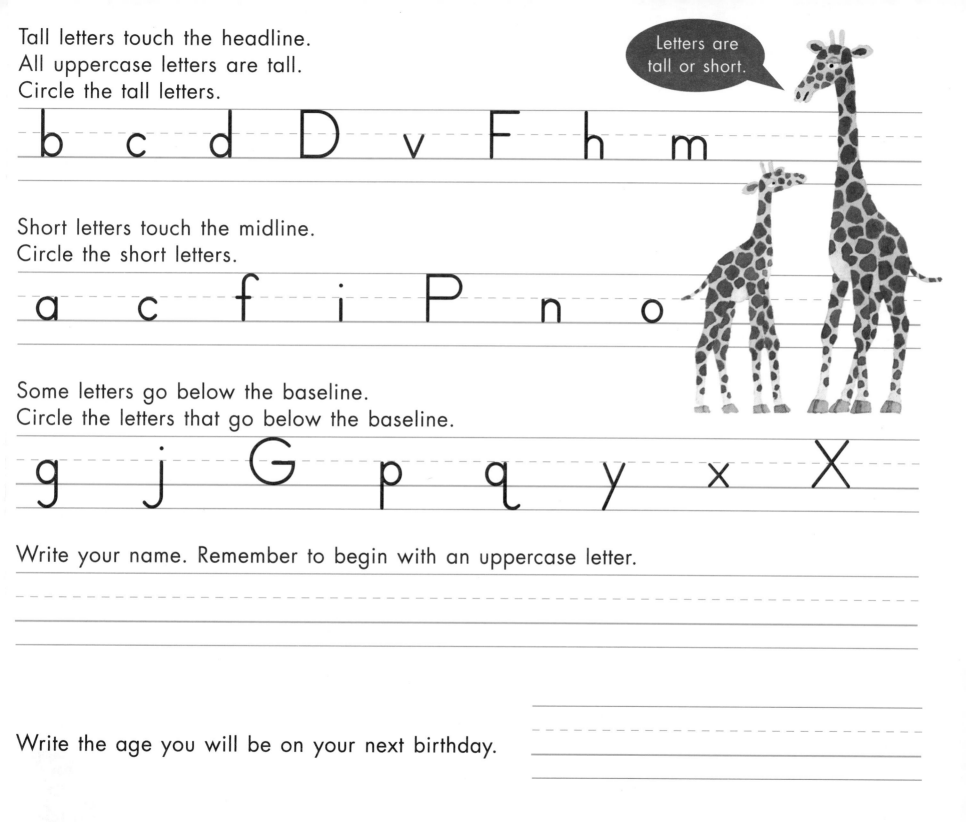

Letters are tall or short.

Pull Down Straight Lines

Trace each pull down straight line.

L   h   I   l   i   T   n   5   g

Write these letters and numerals.

a   B   d   t   E   9   r   H   4   F

Write these sentences.

I like to write.

This is my best writing.

Circle the letters with pull down straight lines.

Slide Right and Slide Left Lines

Trace each slide right and slide left line.

L F H I G 7 t e 2

Write these letters and numerals.

e f t E 2 J H T G Z 5

Write these sentences.

September is a fall month.

Winter starts in December.

Circle the letters with slide right lines.

Circle Lines

Trace each circle line.

C 8 e a O b g d p

Write these letters and numerals.

o S s p 6 3 c D h Q

Write these sentences.

Pizza tastes good.

Peanut butter is better.

Circle the letters with circle lines.

Slant Lines

Trace each slant line.

W Q A y X v w k 7

Write these letters and numerals.

w Y V K Z x M N y 7 2

Write these sentences.

My favorite color is green.

Blue and yellow make green.

Circle the letters with slant lines.

Before You Go On . . .

Circle one word in each line.

This writing is easy to read.

```
D F H I L M J
W Q C A N G H
P W R I T E V
L E T T E R S
```

Write the message.

_____

- -

_____

_____

Writing in Manuscript

In the pages that follow, you will learn ways to make your writing easy for you and for others to read. You will review all lowercase and uppercase letters and use them to write words.

Keys to Legibility: Size and Shape

Let's look at size and shape.

These letters are just right.

I love puzzles.

The tall letters touch the headline.
The short letters touch the midline.
Some short letters go below the baseline.

Letters have 4 kinds of lines.

Look at the models. Write each letter.
Then circle each letter with correct size and shape.

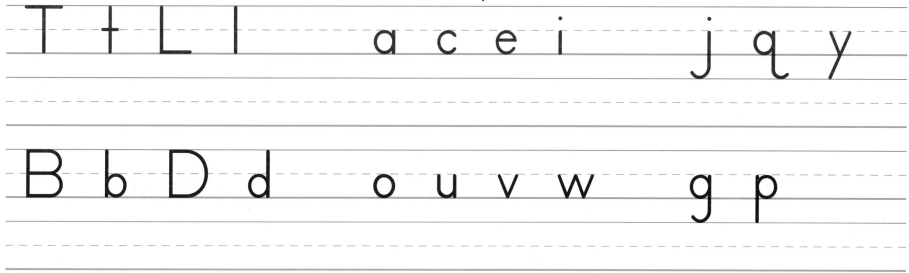

T t L l   a c e i   j q y

B b D d   o u v w   g p

Keys to Legibility: Slant

Let's look at slant.

These letters are just right.

I love to pretend.

The letters are straight up and down.

Look at letters with pull down straight strokes.

Look at the models. Write each word.
Then circle each word in which the letters are straight up and down.

sing   act   dance   shout

jump   twirl   skip   clap

Keys to Legibility: Spacing

Let's look at spacing.

These words are just right.

I love jokes.

The letters are not too close.
The letters are not too far apart.
There is a finger space between words.

Look at the models. Write each word.
Then circle each word with correct letter spacing.

silly   funny   cute   long

Put a star next to the sentence with good word spacing.
Then write the sentence correctly.

I know a joke.   I know a joke.

Trace and write the letters.

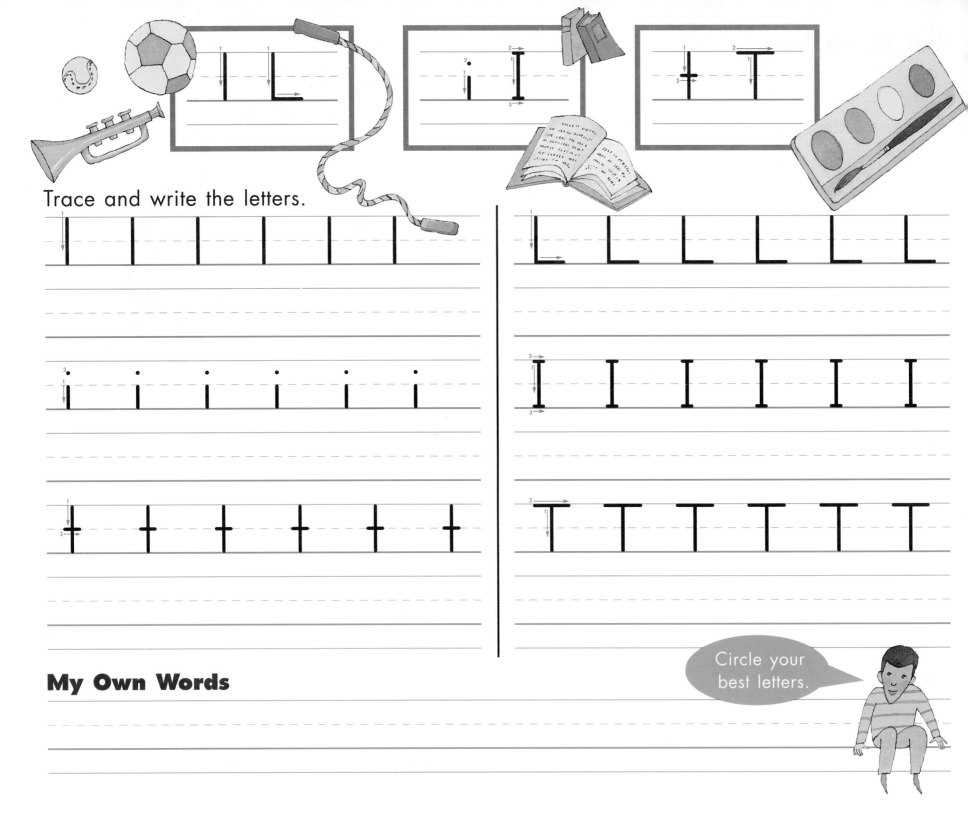

My Own Words

Write names of people.

Lela

Ira

Tim

Ilse

Luis

Tatiana

On Your Own Write your full name.

Circle the name you wrote best.

21

Trace and write the letters.

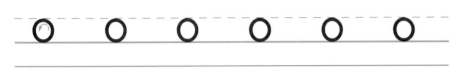

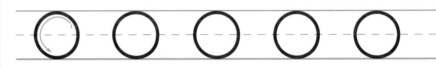

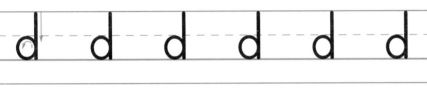

My Own Words

Circle your best letters.

Begin each name with an uppercase letter.

Write names of cities.

Oakland

Akron

Dallas

Atlanta

Orlando

Detroit

On Your Own

Write the name of the town or city and the state where you live.

Circle the name you wrote best.

Trace and write the letters.

c c c c c c

C C C C C C

e e e e e e

E E E E E E

f f f f f f

F F F F F F

Circle your best letters.

My Own Words

Begin important words in each title with an uppercase letter.

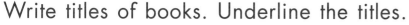

Write titles of books. Underline the titles.

Clifford's Family

Caps for Sale

Ernest and Celestine's Picnic

On Your Own Write the title of a book you like.

Circle the title you wrote best.

25

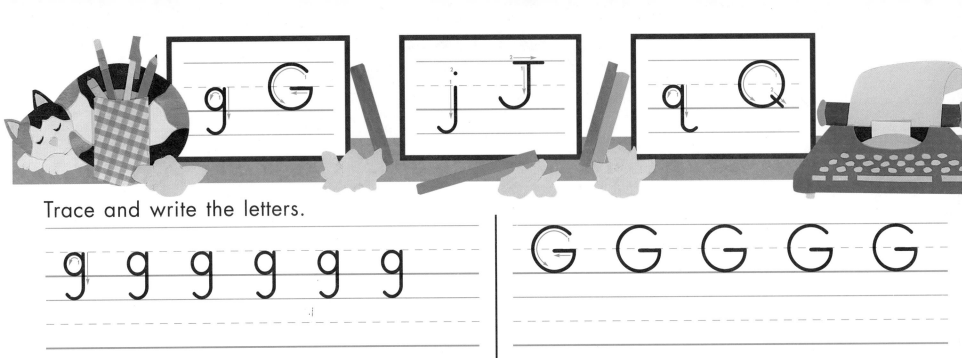

Trace and write the letters.

g g g g g g   G G G G G

j j j j j j   J J J J J

q q q q q q   Q Q Q Q Q

My Own Words

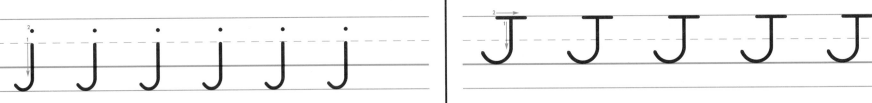

Circle your best letters.

Begin each name with an uppercase letter.

Write first and last names of authors.

Gail Gibbons

Angela Johnson

Robert Quackenbush

On Your Own Write the name of an author whose book you like.

Circle the name you wrote best.

Trace and write the numerals.

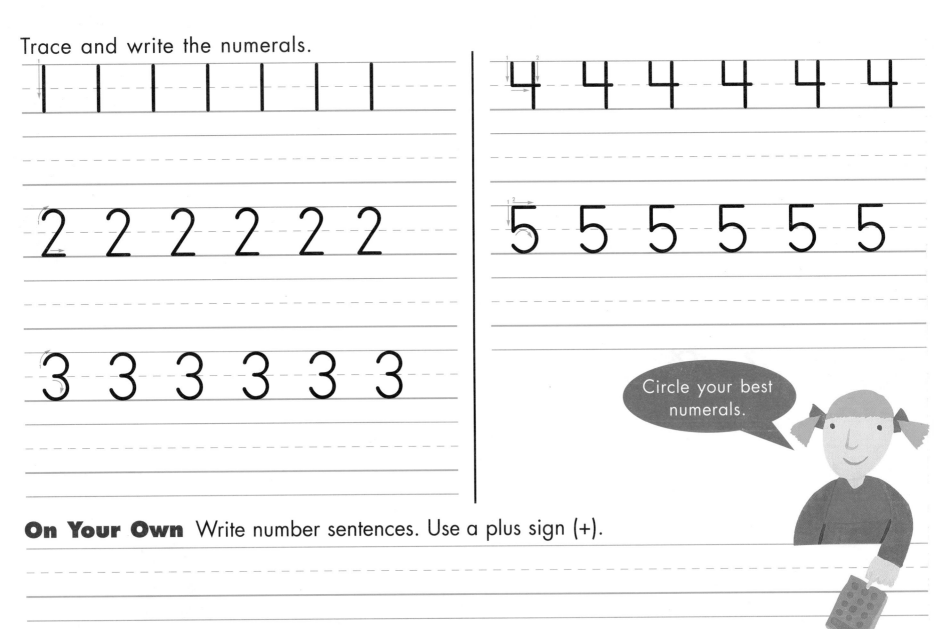

1 1 1 1 1 1 1

2 2 2 2 2 2 2

3 3 3 3 3 3 3

4 4 4 4 4 4

5 5 5 5 5 5 5

Circle your best numerals.

On Your Own Write number sentences. Use a plus sign (+).

28

| 6 | 7 | 8 | 9 | 10 |

Trace and write the numerals.

6 6 6 6 6 6 6

7 7 7 7 7 7 7

8 8 8 8 8 8

9 9 9 9 9 9 9

10 10 10 10 10

On Your Own Write number sentences. Use a minus sign (–).

Circle your best numerals.

9-7

u U   s S

Trace and write the letters.

u u u u u u

U U U U U U

s s s s s s

S S S S S S

Circle your best letters.

My Own Words

30

Begin important words in each title with an uppercase letter.

Write titles of songs. Use quotation marks— " and ".

"Six Little Ducks"

"When You Wish Upon a Star"

"Under the Sea"   "Sing"

On Your Own Write the title of a song you like to sing.

Circle the title you wrote best.

b B   p P   r R

Trace and write the letters.

b b b b b b   B B B B B

p p p p p p   P P P P P

r r r r r r   R R R R R

Circle your best letters.

My Own Words

32

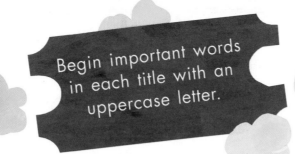

Begin important words in each title with an uppercase letter.

Write titles of movies. Underline the titles.

The Red Balloon

Beauty and the Beast

Pinocchio   Peter Pan

Circle the title you wrote best.

On Your Own Write the title of a movie you like.

33

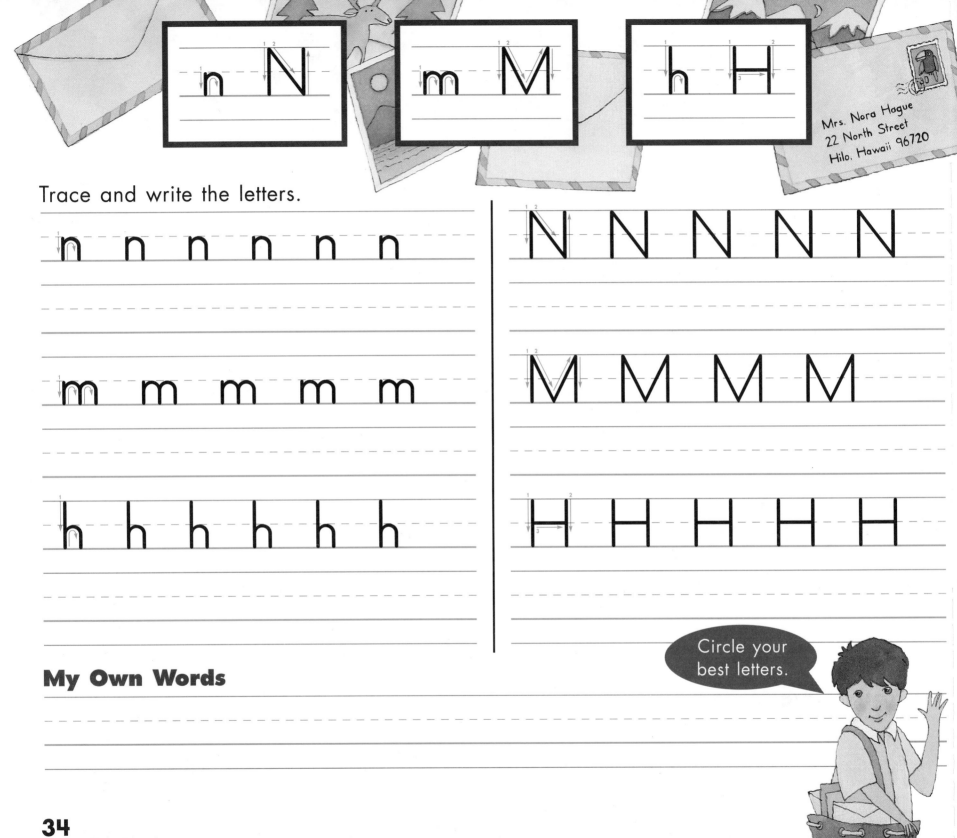

Trace and write the letters.

n N   m M   h H

Mrs. Nora Hague
22 North Street
Hilo, Hawaii 96720

n n n n n n

N N N N N

m m m m m

M M M M

h h h h h h

H H H H H

My Own Words

Circle your
best letters.

34

Write special titles and names of people.

Mr. Herman Nunez

Major Helen Harris

Ms. Michelle Needham

On Your Own Write the name of one of your teachers.

Circle the name you wrote best.

35

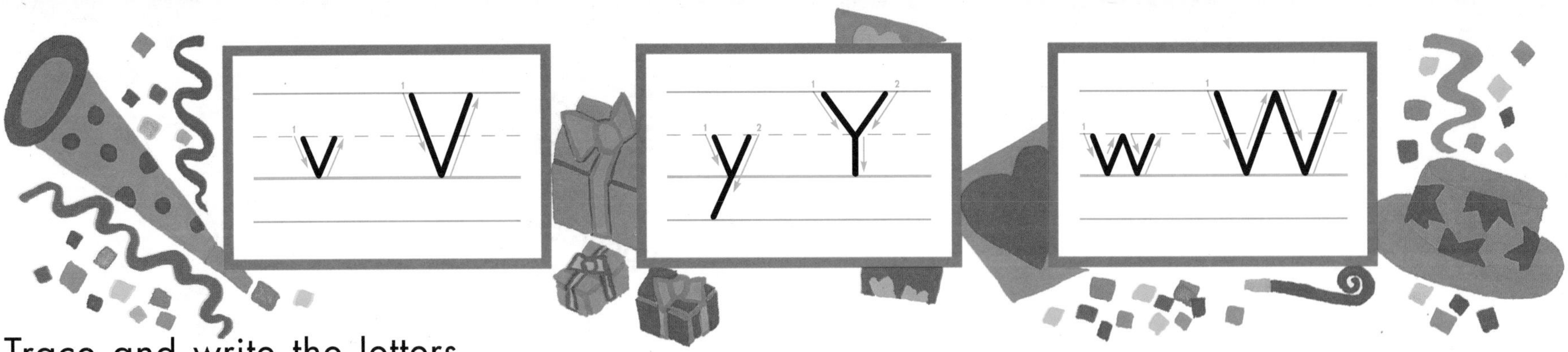

v V   y Y   w W

Trace and write the letters.

v V V V V V   V V V V V

y y y y y y   Y Y Y Y Y

w w w w w   W W W W W

My Own Words

Circle your best letters.

36

Begin each word with an uppercase letter.

Write names of holidays. Put an apostrophe (') in each one.

New Year's Eve

Valentine's Day

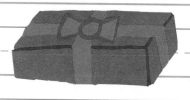

Washington's Birthday

On Your Own Write about a holiday you like to celebrate.

Circle the holiday you wrote best.

37

Trace and write the letters.

x x x x x x x

X X X X X X

k k k k k k k

K K K K K K

z z z z z z z

Z Z Z Z Z Z

My Own Words

Circle your best letters.

Write signs.

Shh! Children Snoozing!

Keep Off the Grass!   EXIT

Quiet Zone!   No Parking

On Your Own Write a sign for your classroom.

Circle the sign you wrote best.

39

Show What You Can Do

Write some names you like.

_____

- -

_____

Write the title of a movie you would like to see.

_____

- -

_____

Write the title of a song you sing in school.

_____

- -

_____

Write the title of a book you read.

_____

- -

_____

Write a sign you might see in a school library.

_____

Circle your best word.

- -

_____

Draw a picture of a place you would like to visit.
Then write a story to go with your picture.

Put a star next to
your best sentence.

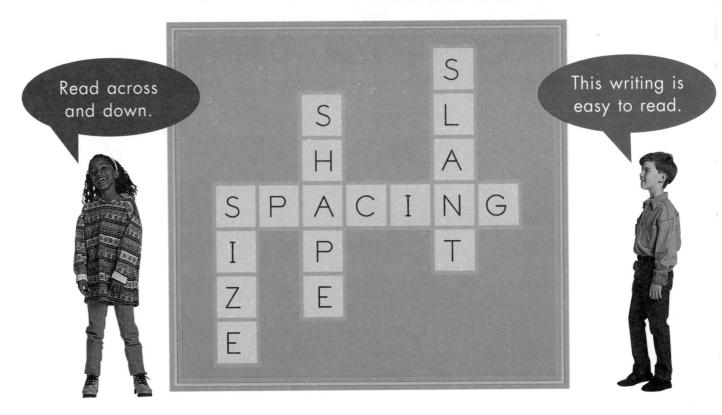

Read across and down.

This writing is easy to read.

S
H
S P A C I N G
I P
Z E
E

S
L
A
N
T

Write the words that name the keys to legibility.
Write size and shape on the first line.

_____

_____

_____   _____

_____   _____

Keys to Legibility

In the following pages, you will look at the size
and shape, slant, and spacing of your writing.
You will find many interesting things to write.

Keys to Legibility: Size and Shape

Make your writing easy to read.
Look at the size and shape of your letters.

hamster  rabbit goldfish cat

Write these words. Make sure your tall letters touch the headline.

lion  bear  zebra  mouse

Write these words. Make sure your short letters touch the midline.

jaguar  penguin quail

Write these words. Make sure letters that go below
the baseline touch the next line.

Are your words easy to read?

43

Copy Cats

hiss	jump	meow	purr
scratch	sleep	stretch	yowl

Write things cats do.
Use words from the box or other words.

Do your tall letters touch the headline?

On Your Own

What do you think cats like to do most? Write about it.

Circle your best word.

My Hero

lettuce

salami

bologna

tomato

turkey

cheese

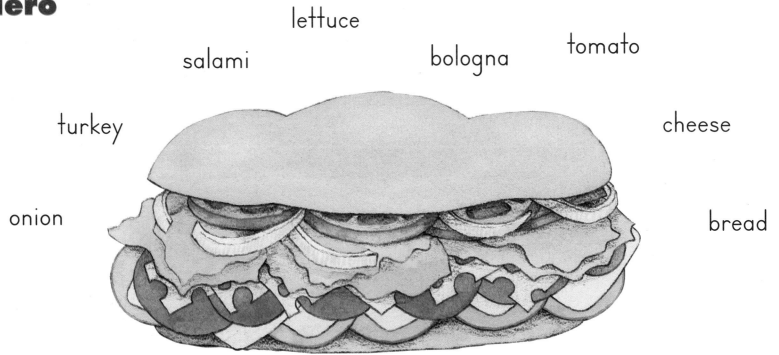

onion

bread

Write what you see in the hero sandwich.

Do your short letters touch the midline?

On Your Own

Tell how you would make a hero sandwich.

Circle your best word.

47

Size and Shape
Frogs and Toads

fire-bellied toad

duck-billed frog

painted reed frog

golden frog

Write the name of each frog and toad.

Does each g go below the baseline?

On Your Own

Make up a name for this frog. Write a story about its life.

Circle your best word.

Word Fun

Follow the directions to complete the word box.

1. Write f in box 1.
2. Write p in box 9.
3. Write a in box 4.
4. Write i in box 8.
5. Write n in box 3.
6. Write r in box 7.
7. Write a in box 6.
8. Write u in box 2.
9. Leave box 5 blank.

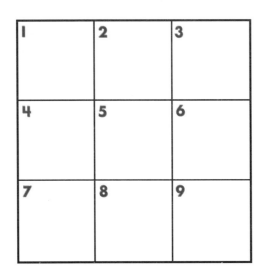

Are your letters easy to read?

Read across and down.
Write the four words you have spelled.

Use the letters to write as many words as you can.

a   b   d   e   i   n   s   t   u

What words can you make from the letters in your name?

Review

ABC's and vegetable goop.
What will I find
in the alphabet soup?
Start with letter a.

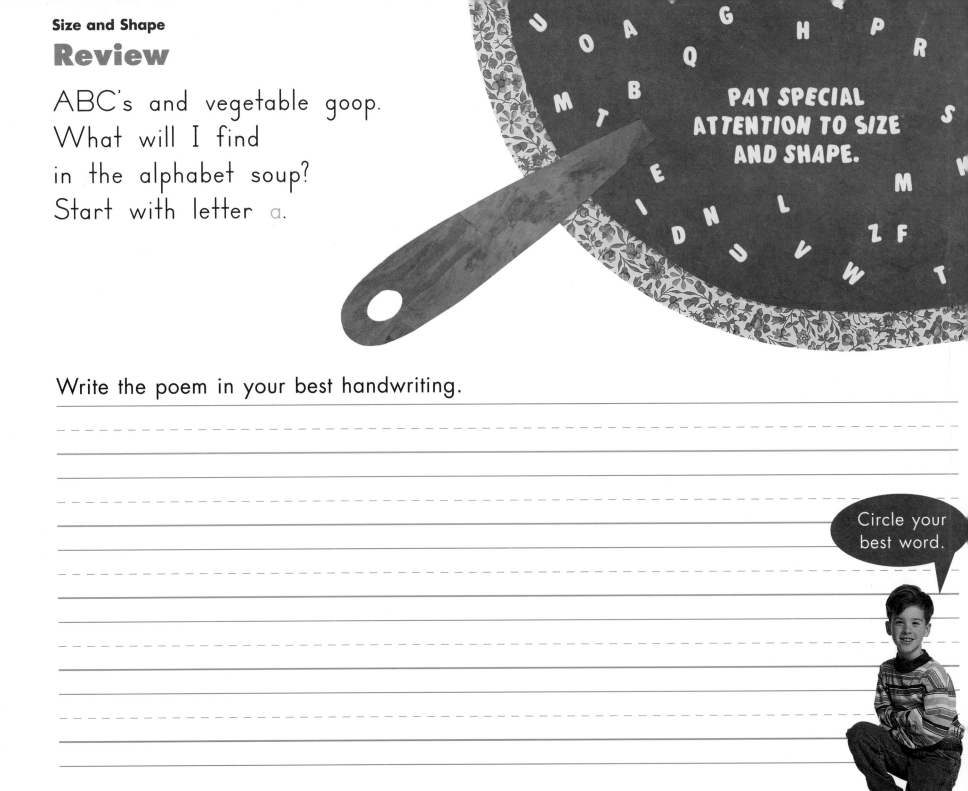

PAY SPECIAL
ATTENTION TO SIZE
AND SHAPE.

Write the poem in your best handwriting.

Circle your
best word.

52

Keys to Legibility: Slant

Make your writing easy to read.
Look at the slant of your letters.

1. Position your paper properly.
2. Pull downstrokes in the right direction.
3. Shift your paper as you write.

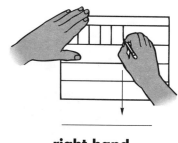

left hand   **right hand**

Write these words.
Make sure your pull down straight strokes are straight up and down.

imagine    think 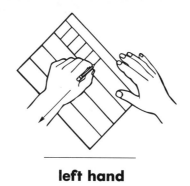   talk    write

read    giggle   build

Are your words easy to read?

53

Be a Clown

baggy   big   floppy   funny

red   silly   striped   tiny

Write words that describe clowns.
Use words from the box or other words.

Did you position your paper properly?

On Your Own

If you dressed like a clown, what would you look like?
Draw a picture and describe it.

Circle a word in which your letters are straight up and down.

Inside Out

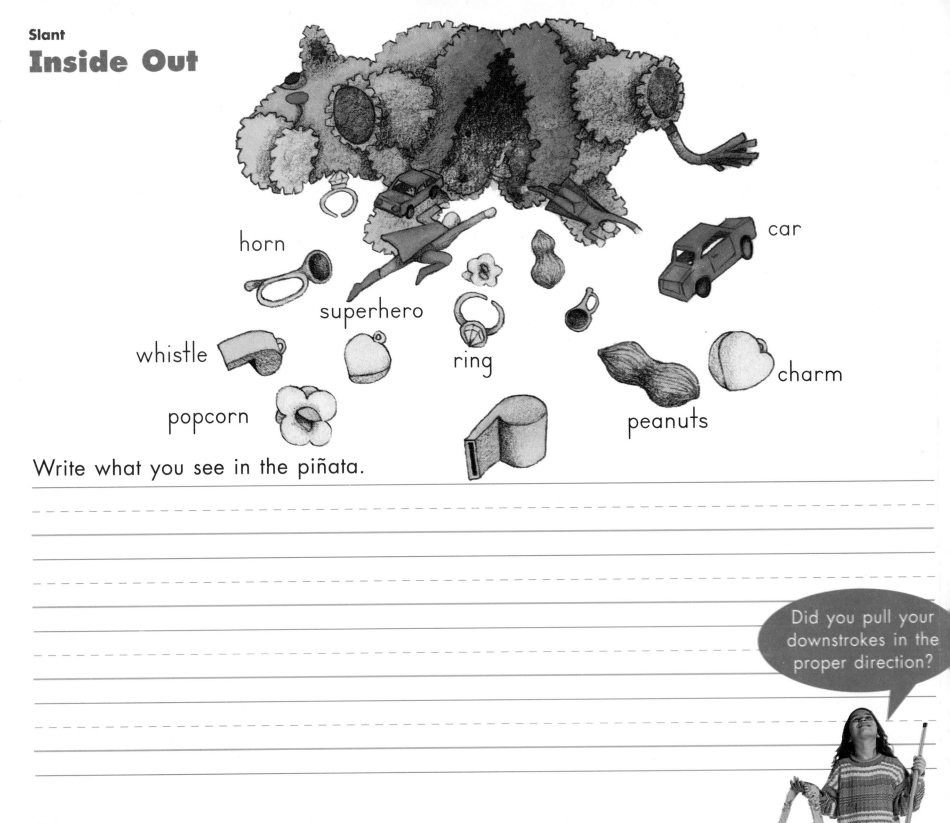

horn

superhero

whistle

ring

charm

car

popcorn

peanuts

Write what you see in the piñata.

Did you pull your downstrokes in the proper direction?

On Your Own

Write what you would put in a piñata.

Circle a word in which your letters are straight up and down.

57

Creeping Crawlers

lacewing fly

green shield bug

praying mantis

net-winged beetle

Write the name of each insect.

Did you shift your paper as you wrote?

On Your Own

Imagine you are this insect. Tell what you do each day.

Circle a word in which your letters are straight up and down.

In Other Words

Write the words that name the baked food.

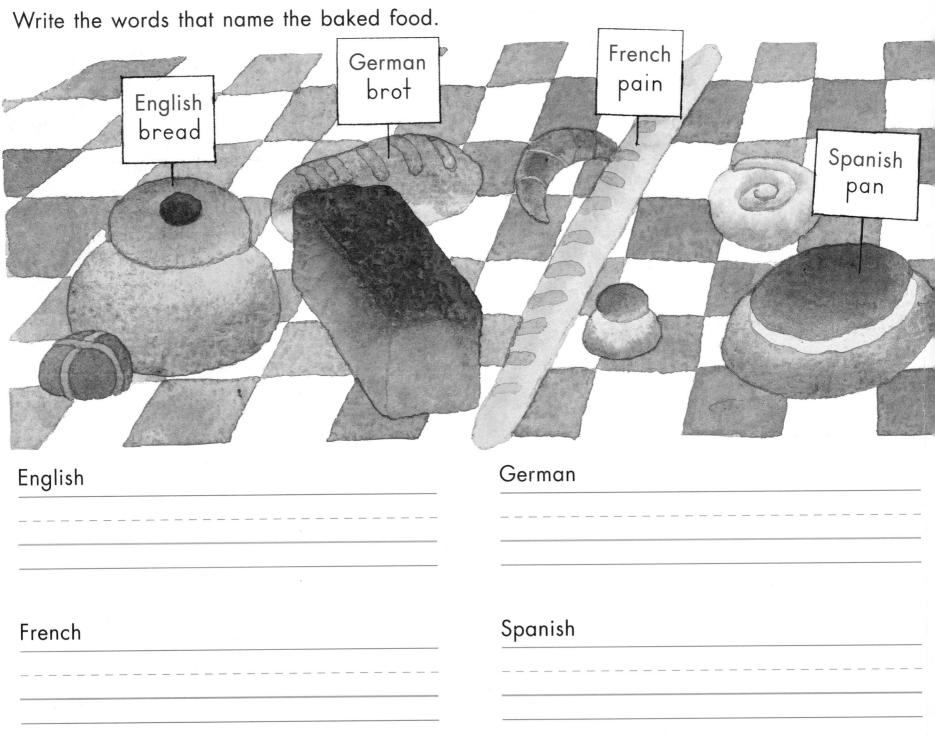

English

_____

- - - - - - - - - - - - - - - -

_____

German

_____

- - - - - - - - - - - - - - - -

_____

French

_____

- - - - - - - - - - - - - - - -

_____

Spanish

_____

- - - - - - - - - - - - - - - -

_____

60

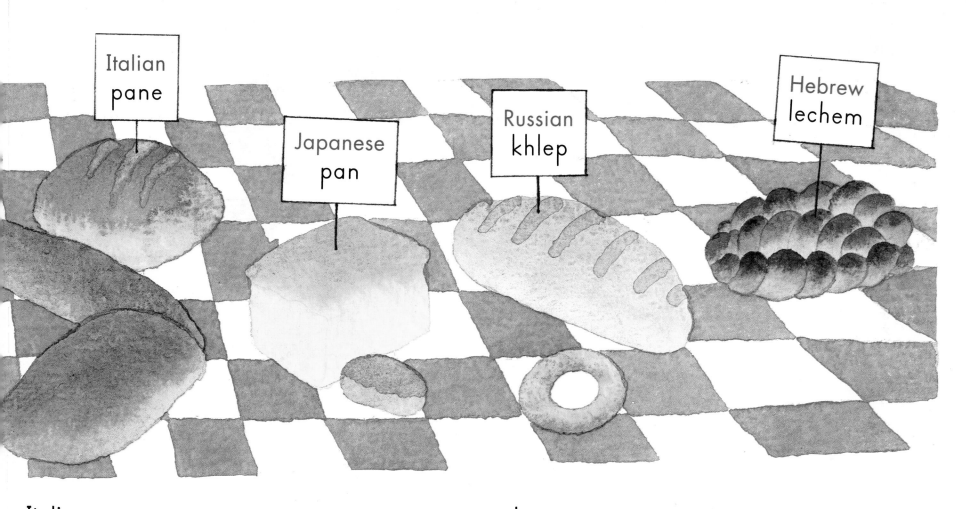

Italian

_____

- - - - - - - - - - - -

_____

Japanese

_____

- - - - - - - - - - - -

_____

Russian

_____

- - - - - - - - - - - -

_____

Hebrew

_____

- - - - - - - - - - - -

_____

61

Review

Jump rope, jump rope,
Just watch this!
Jump rope, jump rope,
I can't miss!

Pay special attention to slant.

Write the poem in your best handwriting.

Circle a word in which your letters are straight up and down.

Keys to Legibility: Spacing

Make your writing easy to read.
Look at the spacing between letters and words.

These letters are too close.

Miguel

These letters are too far apart.

Mary

Write these names.
Make sure your spacing is just right.

Samuel

Teiko

There should be a finger space between words. Write the sentence.

Miguel and Mary read rhymes.

Is your sentence easy to read?

Meet Mother Goose Characters

Bo-Peep	Humpty Dumpty	Jack	Jill
King Cole	Miss Muffet	Mother Goose	Simple Simon

Write names of nursery rhyme characters.
Use names from the box or other names.

Is your
letter spacing
correct?

On Your Own

Which nursery rhyme character would you like to meet? Tell why.

Circle a word with correct letter spacing.

The Best Nest

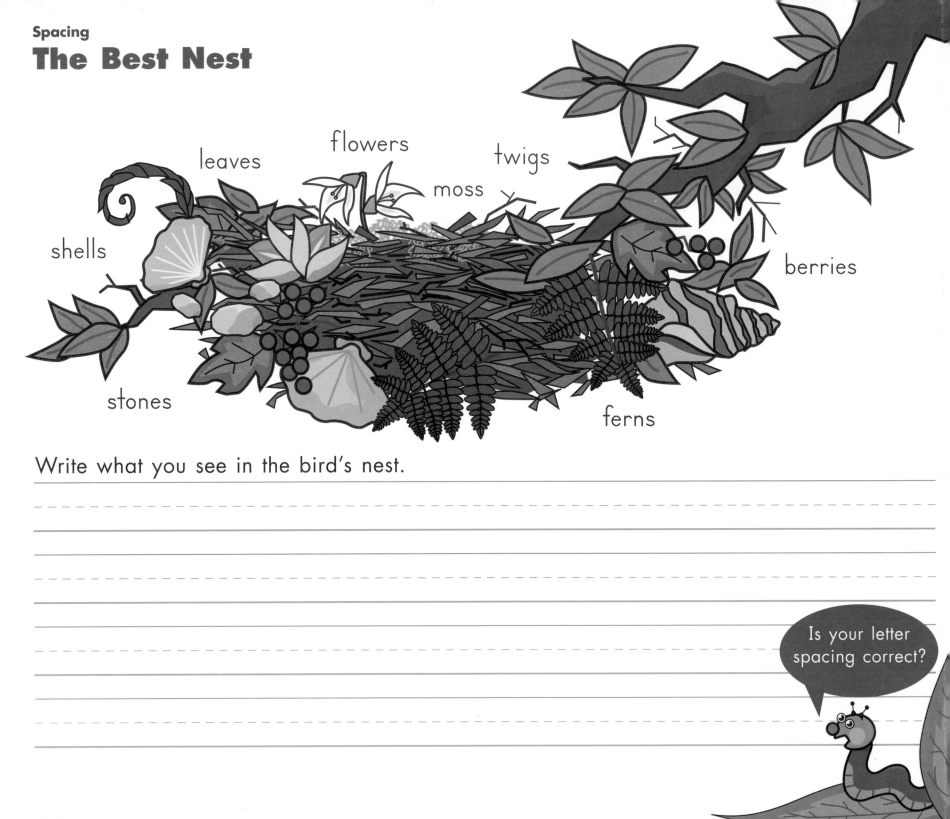

leaves
flowers
twigs
moss
shells
berries
stones
ferns

Write what you see in the bird's nest.

Is your letter spacing correct?

On Your Own

Write what you would use to make a nest.

Circle a word with correct letter spacing.

Feathered Friends

hornbill

Write the name of each bird.

emerald cuckoo

tufted puffin

Is your letter spacing correct?

stilt

On Your Own

Describe this bird. Make up a name for it.

Put a star next to a sentence with good word spacing.

Review

Mabel, Mabel, set the table,
Just as fast as you are able.
Salt, sugar, vinegar,
mustard, red-hot pepper!

Pay special attention to spacing.

Write the poem in your best handwriting.

Put a star next to a line with good word spacing.

Keys to Legibility: Size and Shape

Let's look at size and shape again.

dog 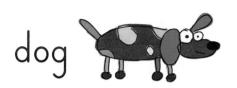 parrot snail newt

Write these words. Make sure your straight lines are straight.

cow  goat  chick  duck

Write these words. Make sure your circle lines are round.

gopher  porcupine squirrel

Write these words.
Make sure lines that go below the baseline touch the next headline.

Are your words easy to read?

A Dog's Life

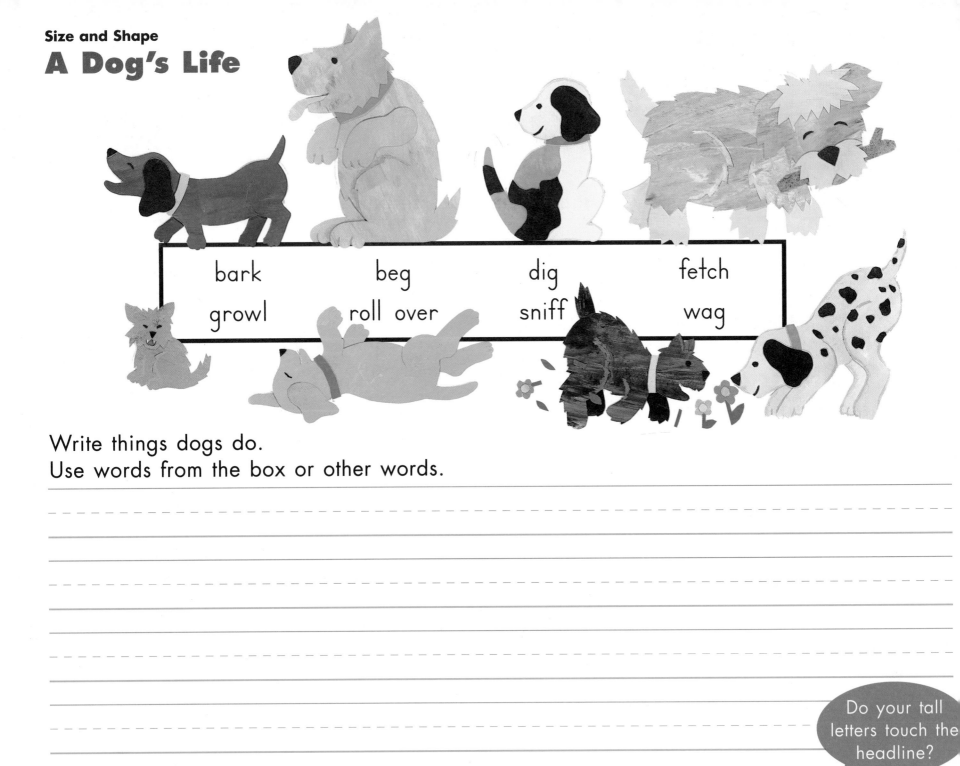

bark   beg   dig   fetch

growl   roll over   sniff   wag

Write things dogs do.
Use words from the box or other words.

Do your tall letters touch the headline?

On Your Own

What do you think dogs like to do most? Write about it.

Circle your best word.

Stone Soup

lima beans

carrots

tomatoes

stone

onions

water

celery

barley

Write what can go in a pot of soup.

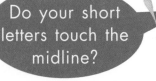

Do your short letters touch the midline?

On Your Own

Write what you would put in a pot of stone soup.
Don't forget the stone!

Circle your best word.

Hairy Mammals

duck-billed platypus

three-toed sloth

wrinkle-faced bat

star-nosed mole

Write the name of each mammal.

Does each p go below the baseline?

On Your Own

Write about how this mammal might protect itself.

Circle your best word.

Number Fun

Add the numbers to complete the number square.

Add +	9	8	7	6	5
1	10				
2					7
3				9	
4		12			
5				11	10

Use the number line to help you.

Color all the 10's. How many do you see? _____

Write the numerals from 1 to 9 in the boxes.

☐ ☐ ☐ ☐ ☐ ☐ ☐ ☐ ☐

Finish the magic squares.
Each row across and down should add up to 15.
Each square should have every number from 1 to 9 in it.

4		
		7
8	1	

1		5
		7
8		

Review

What shall I name
my little pup?
I'll have to think
a good name up.
Start with letter A.

Pay special attention
to size and shape.

Write the poem in your best handwriting.

Circle your
best word.

80

Keys to Legibility: Slant

Let's look at slant again.

Here's a good way to check your letters.
Draw lines through the pull down straight strokes.

If the lines you drew stand up straight, your word has correct slant.

bananas   strawberries

Write these words. Draw lines to check your slant.

I like apple pie.

Write this sentence. Draw lines to check your slant.

Are your letters straight up and down?

The Wishing Tree

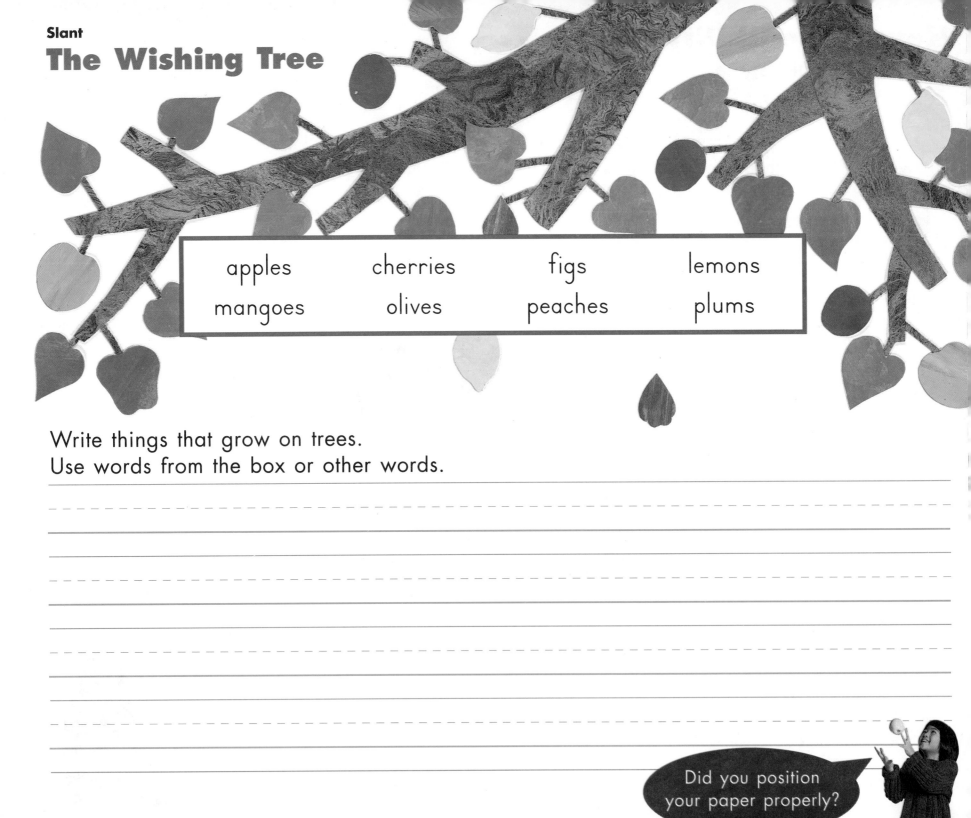

apples	cherries	figs	lemons
mangoes	olives	peaches	plums

Write things that grow on trees.
Use words from the box or other words.

Did you position your paper properly?

On Your Own

What do you wish would grow on a tree?
Draw a picture and write about it.

Circle a word in which your letters are straight up and down.

83

Beans and Peas and Carrots Grow

lettuce   squash   eggplant   string beans

tomato   cucumber   carrots   sweet peas

Write what you see in a vegetable garden.

Did you pull your downstrokes in the proper direction?

On Your Own

Tell how you would plant a vegetable garden.

Circle a word in which your letters are straight up and down.

85

Leaping Lizards

beaded lizard

six-lined race runner

blue-tongued skink

frilled lizard

Write the name of each reptile.

Did you shift your paper as you wrote?

On Your Own

Make up a name for this lizard. Write about it.

Circle a word in which your letters are straight up and down.

The Name of the Game

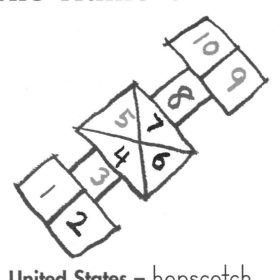

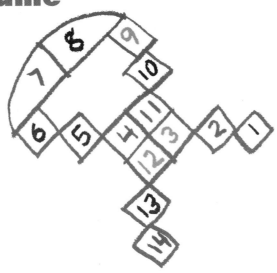

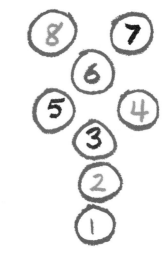

United States – hopscotch   **Italy –** campana   **Nigeria –** ta galagala

Write the name of each game.

Country   Game

Italy

Nigeria

United States

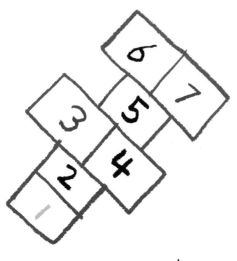 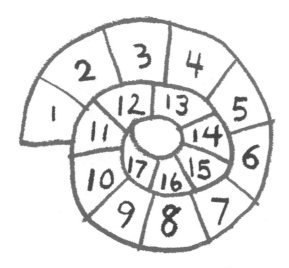 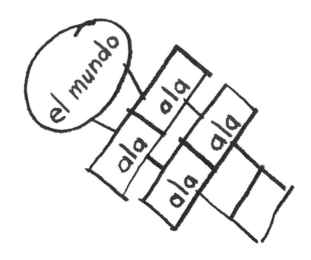

Trinidad – jumby   **France** – escargot   **El Salvador** – peregrina

Write the name of each game.

Country   Game

El Salvador

France

Trinidad

Review

Jelly in the bowl,
Jelly in the bowl.
Wiggle, waggle,
Wiggle, waggle,
Jelly in the bowl.

Pay special attention to slant.

Write the poem in your best handwriting.

Circle a word in which your letters are straight up and down.

Keys to Legibility: Spacing

Let's look at spacing again.

Look for letters and words that are too close or too far apart.
There should be enough space for an index finger to fit between words.

Sometimes I help at home.

Find the mistakes in each sentence. Write the sentences correctly.

I cleanmyroom.

I hang   up my cl ot hes.

I put   awaym yto ys.

Are your sentences easy to read?

91

Lend a Hand

| make the bed | rake leaves | set the table |
| shovel snow | dry the dishes | water the plants |

Write how you can help at home.
Use words from the box or other words.

Is there enough space between your words?

On Your Own

If you had a robot, what would you want it to do to help you? Write about it.

Put a star next to a sentence with good word spacing.

It's About Time

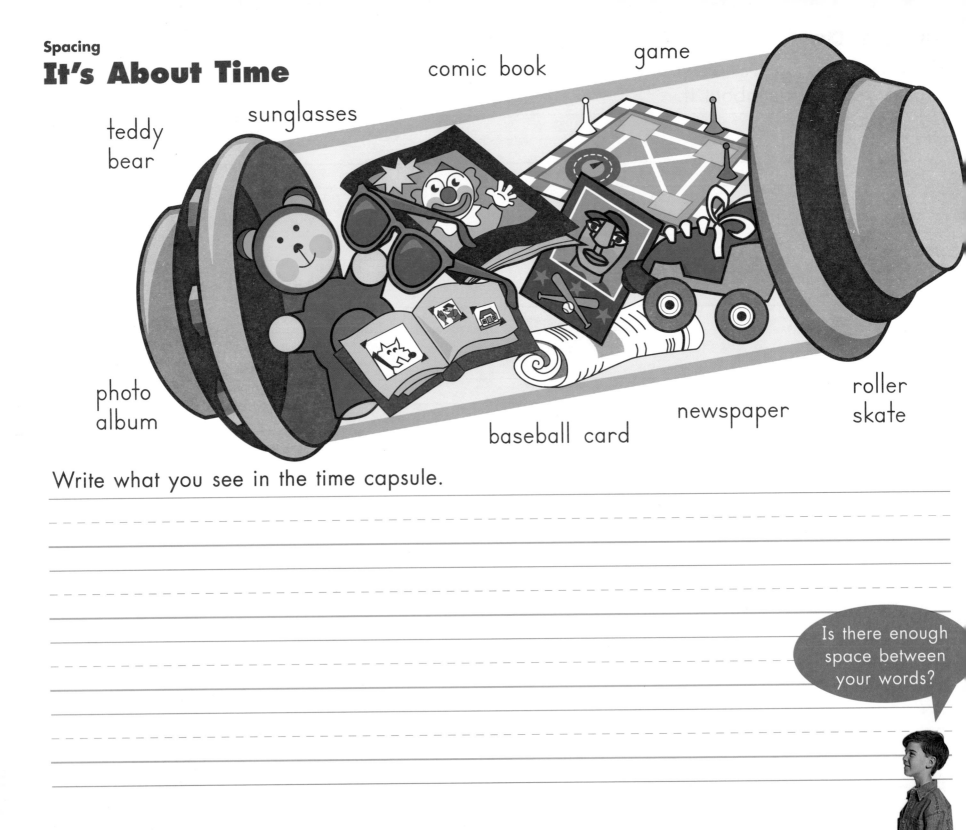

teddy bear

sunglasses

comic book

game

photo album

baseball card

newspaper

roller skate

Write what you see in the time capsule.

Is there enough space between your words?

On Your Own

Write what you would put in a time capsule.

Put a star next to an example of good word spacing.

95

Under the Sea

puffer fish

porcupine fish

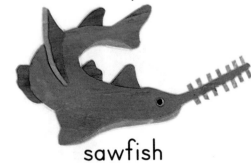

butterfly fish

sawfish

Write the name of each fish.

Is your letter spacing correct?

On Your Own

Make up a name for this fish. Write a story about it.

Put a star next to a sentence with good letter spacing.

Review

Teddy bear, teddy bear,
Turn around.
Teddy bear, teddy bear,
Touch the ground.

Teddy bear, teddy bear,
Show your shoe.
Teddy bear, teddy bear,
That will do.

Write a word that has three tall letters.

Write a word that has all short letters.

Write the word will.
Make sure the letters are straight up and down.

Write a six-letter word with correct letter spacing.

Teddy bear, teddy bear,
Turn out the light.
Teddy bear, teddy bear,
Say good night.

Pay attention to size and shape, slant, and spacing.

Write this verse in your best handwriting.

Put a star next to your best line of writing.

I Can

I can write a story.

I can write a poem.

I can write at school,

And I can write at home.

I Can
I can write a story.
I can write a poem.
I can write at school,
And I can write at home.

I Can
I can write a story.
I can write a poem.
I can write at school,
And I can write at home.

I Can
I can write a story.
I can write a poem.
I can write at school,
And I can write at home.

I Can

I can write a story.
I can write a poem.
I can write at school,
And I can write at home.

Write the poem in your best handwriting.
Pay attention to size and shape, slant, and spacing.

Put a star next to your best line of writing.

101

Record of Student's Handwriting Skills

Manuscript

	Needs Improvement	Shows Mastery
Positions paper correctly	☐	☐
Holds pencil correctly	☐	☐
Writes pull down straight lines	☐	☐
Writes slide right and slide left lines	☐	☐
Writes circle lines	☐	☐
Writes slant lines	☐	☐
Writes l and L	☐	☐
Writes i and I	☐	☐
Writes t and T	☐	☐
Writes o and O	☐	☐
Writes a and A	☐	☐
Writes d and D	☐	☐
Writes c and C	☐	☐
Writes e and E	☐	☐
Writes f and F	☐	☐
Writes g and G	☐	☐
Writes j and J	☐	☐
Writes q and Q	☐	☐

	Needs Improvement	Shows Mastery
Writes numerals **1–10**	☐	☐
Writes **u** and **U**	☐	☐
Writes **s** and **S**	☐	☐
Writes **b** and **B**	☐	☐
Writes **p** and **P**	☐	☐
Writes **r** and **R**	☐	☐
Writes **n** and **N**	☐	☐
Writes **m** and **M**	☐	☐
Writes **h** and **H**	☐	☐
Writes **v** and **V**	☐	☐
Writes **y** and **Y**	☐	☐
Writes **w** and **W**	☐	☐
Writes **x** and **X**	☐	☐
Writes **k** and **K**	☐	☐
Writes **z** and **Z**	☐	☐
Writes with correct size and shape	☐	☐
Writes with correct slant	☐	☐
Writes with correct spacing	☐	☐
Regularly checks written work for legibility	☐	☐

Index